how to live a
mindful
life

how to live a
mindful
life

ONE HUNDRED WAYS TO
A CENTRED LIFE

Bounty
BOOKS

An Hachette UK Company
www.hachette.co.uk

First published as *Everyday Mindfulness* in 2016 by
Bounty Books, a division of
Octopus Publishing Group Ltd
Carmelite House
50 Victoria Embankment
London, EC4Y 0DZ
www.octopusbooks.co.uk

ISBN: 978-0-7537-3283-0

A CIP catalogue record for this book is available
from the British Library

Printed and bound in China

10 9 8 7 6 5 4 3 2 1

Publisher: Lucy Pessell
Designer: Lisa Layton
Editor: Sarah Vaughan
Production Controller: Beata Kibil
Images: Shutterstock/Irtsya

INTRODUCTION

Mindful (adjective):
Fully aware of the moment, whilst self-conscious and attentive to this awareness.

"He became mindful of the warm fire, in the frost of winter."

How to Live a Mindful Life provides a mindful exercise, idea, or inspirational quote for every day of the year. Adopting a mindful lifestyle doesn't have to mean taking hours out of your day to meditate.

In fact, every situation you find yourself in presents an opportunity to practise mindfulness: waiting at the bus stop, queuing in a shop, even performing household chores…

Just taking a few minutes each day to ground yourself in the present moment can be hugely beneficial to both your physical and mental well-being.

Increasingly, research is suggesting that mindfulness can lower stress levels and blood pressure, improve your quality of sleep, and so much more.

Developing the habit of daily mindfulness will likely improve your overall quality of life and your levels of happiness, as well as bringing a sense of inner peace.

Mindfulness can feel counterintuitive to our usual way. We are busy, so we rush. We have too much to do, so we multitask. Conversely, to be mindful is to slow down and focus on one task at a time.

You will actually improve your productivity if you can manage to do this and you will certainly live your life with a greater sense of calm.

To be mindful is to learn how to fully appreciate life's little pleasures and the most precious of moments that all too often pass by unnoticed when the mind is distracted.

Don't let another year slip through your fingers in the blink of an eye. Use this book as your guide, inspiration, and motivation to embrace a year of mindful living.

THE BODY SCAN

The body scan meditation is a great place to start your mindfulness journey:

Make yourself comfortable, lying on your back on the floor or on your bed. Allow your eyes to close gently. Take a few moments to get in touch with the movement of your breath and the sensations in your body. When you are ready, begin by focusing your attention on the tips of your toes and then move up the body slowly, focusing on each body part as you go; the ball and heel of the foot. The sides and upper part of the foot. The ankle…As you breathe in, imagine the breath going down your body and into your toes. As you breathe out, imagine the breath going back up your body and out of your nose. Repeat this process of gentle awareness of each body part and sensation until you reach the top of your head.

"If you want to conquer the anxiety of life, live in the moment, live in the breath."

– AMIT RAY

"Mindfulness is simply being aware of what is happening right now without wishing it were different; enjoying the pleasant without holding on when it changes (which it will); being with the unpleasant without fearing it will always be this way (which it won't)."

– JAMES BARAZ

MINDFUL
COMMUNICATION

Today, practise bringing your mindful attention to your interactions
with others. Focus on making eye contact with the people you
communicate with, on really seeing them.

"Respond; don't react.
Listen; don't talk.
Think; don't assume."

– RAJI LUKKOOR

WAKE UP GENTLY

Try keeping your eyes closed for a few minutes after you wake. Focus on your breathing and on the sensations around you — the softness of your duvet, the smell of the sheets, distant sounds from outside the window…

TRANSFORMATIONAL LAUNDRY

Transform chores into mindful tasks by slowing them down and really paying attention. When doing the laundry, notice the feel and textures of the fabrics and how fresh they smell. Pay attention to the patterns and colors and the way they are affected by the light of the room. Make folding into a sort of yoga practice and move with mindfulness, attentive to each fold. This keeps you in tune with the moment, with yourself and your space — all functioning in harmony.

"If you are mentally somewhere else, you miss real life."

– BYRON KATIE

"My goal today is to live in a state of grace and lightness. I will not invite struggle or drama. I will say yes more and smile often."

– KIMBERLEY BLAINE

CREATE A "TO-BE" LIST

This is an alternative to a to-do list. Halfway through the day, pause and take a minute to ask, "How am I being right now?" Curt, or understanding? Defensive, or open-minded? Dismissive, or kind? Turn your "to-be" list into a goal and try to maintain it on a discreet post-it on your desk, or wherever you are likely to see it, to keep your intentions in check.

"The present moment is filled with joy and happiness. If you are attentive, you will see it."

– THÍCH NHẤT HẠNH

DO NOTHING

Even if it's just for five minutes, sit for that five minutes and do… nothing. Sit silently in a comfortable chair or in a sunny spot outside, if possible without mobile phones or other distractions near you. Become still. Bring your full awareness into the present moment. All that exists for you is the here and now. You may be amazed at how pleasurable and satisfying it is just to "be", and how much taking just five minutes from your day will give back to your life as a whole.

"Allow yourself to rest. Your soul speaks to you in the quiet moments in between your thoughts."

– ANONYMOUS

MINDFUL WALKING

Walking can give you a chance to spend time being mindful without taking any extra time out of your day. Wherever you are walking to or from today, turn it into a meditative exercise. Walk slowly, paying attention to the sensations on the soles of your feet. Notice as each part of the sole, from heel to toe, touches the ground. Lifting, moving, placing. Lifting, moving, placing. Notice how the body moves as you walk. Walk with awareness. One step at a time. Notice any thoughts that arise and let them be.

"Walk as if you are kissing the Earth with your feet."

– THÍCH NHẤT HẠNH

"Carpe Diem.
Seize the day."

– HORACE

"If you don't love yourself,
you cannot love others. If you have no
compassion for yourself, you cannot
develop compassion for others."

– DALAI LAMA

TAKE 5

Every now and then throughout the day, challenge yourself to find five things that are part of your present experience.

First notice five things that you can see with your eyes. They don't necessarily have to be interesting; it might just be a table, the carpet, or a cup in front of you. The aim is simply to bring your full awareness to your experience now in the present moment.

Then notice five things you can hear. Keep listening until you've distinguished five different sounds.

Then notice five things you can feel with your body. These might be the material of your clothes, a slight breeze or even tension in your neck.

"Don't keep allowing the same things to upset you. Life's too short to live that way."

– JOEL OSTEEN

"To see a world in a grain of sand
and heaven in a wild flower,
Hold infinity in the palm of your hand
and eternity in an hour."

– WILLIAM BLAKE

"Mindfulness is the aware, balanced acceptance of the present experience. It isn't more complicated than that. It is being open to or receiving the present moment, pleasant or unpleasant, just as it is, without either clinging to it or rejecting it."

– SYLVIA BOORSTEIN

"Life isn't as serious
as the mind makes it
out to be."

– ECKHART TOLLE

"The best way to capture moments is to pay attention. This is how we cultivate mindfulness. Mindfulness means being awake. It means knowing what you are doing."

– JON KABAT-ZINN

BE HERE NOW

This great piece of advice comes from the well-known spiritual teacher, Ram Dass.

We should ask ourselves: Where am I?

Answer: Here.

Then ask ourselves: What time is it?

Answer: Now.

Keep repeating until you really feel grounded in the present moment.

"Life can be found only in the present moment. The past is gone, the future is not yet here, and if we do not go back to ourselves in the present moment, we cannot be in touch with life."

– THÍCH NHẤT HẠNH

GET UP EARLY TO WATCH THE SUNRISE

The thought of getting up at the crack of dawn may be far from relaxing for many of us, but if you make the effort to do this you will feel revived and refreshed throughout the day as well as carrying a stronger sense of awareness and inner peace. Contemplate the sunrise, absorb the beauty of its colors, notice every aspect of the changing light, embrace the start of a new day. Whatever tasks lie in the day ahead, for these moments let your thoughts be still.

"Thoughts are slow and deep and golden in the morning."

– JOHN STEINBECK

"Forget about the past. It does not exist, except in your memory. Drop it. And stop worrying about how you're going to get through tomorrow. Life is going on right here, right now – pay attention to that and all will be well."

– NEALE DONALD WALSCH

"The moment one gives close
attention to anything, even
a blade of grass, it becomes
a mysterious, awesome,
indescribably magnificent
world in itself."

– HENRY MILLER

THE MINDFUL
TEA MEDITATION

Wrap both your hands around your mug of tea (or other warm beverage). Focus on the warmth radiating through the mug into your hands and breathe deeply. Notice how comforting it is to hold this warm mug between your hands — soothing and relaxing. Really pay attention and breathe deeply for a couple of minutes. Then take your first sip and savour the taste. Focus your mind on the taste. Be aware of how much you enjoy this drink. How the liquid flows over your tongue and down your throat, leaving this wonderful taste that you so appreciate in your mouth.

"Drink your tea slowly and reverently, as if it is the axis on which the world earth revolves — slowly, evenly, without rushing towards the future; live the actual moment. Only this moment is life."

– THÍCH NHẤT HẠNH

CHANGE
YOUR ROUTINE

Drive a different way to work, reverse the order in which you get ready in the morning, or eat something new for breakfast. It's amazing how revitalizing this simple exercise can be.

"Inner peace is the key: if you have inner peace, the external problems do not affect your deep sense of peace and tranquility. Without this inner peace, no matter how comfortable your life is materially, you may still be worried, disturbed, or unhappy because of circumstances."

– DALAI LAMA

LABEL YOUR WORRIES

When you find yourself worrying about something today, consciously stop and label what you are doing as "just worrying." Then bring your attention back to your breath or simply change the subject of your thinking. Every time you catch yourself worrying, just label it again and change the subject.

"We spend precious hours fearing the inevitable. It would be wise to use that time adoring our families, cherishing our friends, and living our lives."

- MAYA ANGELOU

"If you surrender completely to the moments as they pass, you live more richly those moments."

– ANNE MORROW LINDBERGH

"Sometimes you need to take a break from everyone and spend time alone, to experience, appreciate, and love yourself."

– ROBERT TEW

"Right where you are is where you need to be. Don't fight it! Don't run away from it! Stand firm! Take a deep breath. And another. And another. Now, ask yourself: 'Why is this in my world? What do I need to see?'"

– IYANLA VANZANT

TECH TIMEOUT

Technology brings lots of incredible benefits to our lives, but sometimes we need to switch off in order to quieten our thoughts. Today, empower yourself by taking a break from technology for one hour. Mobile phones included.

"Learn to get in touch with the silence within yourself and know that everything in this life has a purpose."

– ELISABETH KÜBLER-ROSS

A SPACE FOR YOU

Today, create a space in your house that is just for you. A calm haven from both the outside world and the comings and goings of the rest of your household. Choose a few of your favourite items — maybe paintings or photographs that make you feel calm or happy — to decorate the space. Maybe a comfortable chair or cushion to sit on, a scented candle, your favourite book. Whatever makes it feel calm, inviting, and just for you.

"I don't have to chase extraordinary moments to find happiness. It's right in front of me if I'm paying attention and practising gratitude."

– BRENÉ BROWN

HARNESS THE HAND-MIND CONNECTION

One of the physical symptoms of stress is that it pulls the blood out of your toes and fingers and sends it to your internal organs. As a calming practice, immerse your hands in warm water to open up the blood vessels and trick your brain out of its stressful state.

"You must live in the present, launch yourself on every wave, find your eternity in each moment. Fools stand on their island opportunities and look toward another land. There is no other land, there is no other life but this."

– HENRY DAVID THOREAU

"Do every act of your life as though it were the very last act of your life."

– MARCUS AURELIUS

"I change my life when I change my thinking. I am Light. I am Spirit. I am a wonderful, capable being. And it is time for me to acknowledge that I create my own reality with my thoughts. If I want to change my reality, then it is time for me to change my mind."

– LOUISE HAY

"There are always flowers for those who want to see them."

– HENRI MATISSE

OBSERVE YOUR THOUGHTS

To start, focus your attention on your breathing. Simply pay attention
to what it feels like in your body as you breathe slowly in and then
slowly breathe out. Now shift your attention to your thoughts. Try to
view them as simply thoughts — they are only objects in your mind.
They are just events happening inside your mind. Notice them enter
your consciousness, develop, and then float away. You don't have to
hold onto or follow your thoughts. Just let them arise and disappear
on their own.

"If you empty yourself of yesterday's sorrows, you will have much more room for today's joy."

– JENNI YOUNG

MAKE THE EVERYDAY MAGICAL

Find a bit of magic in your day. It may be the sound of the rain, the laughter of a loved one, the clouds in the sky, or a quiet moment alone. Whatever it is — and however small — make the magic moment count. Acknowledge it, appreciate it, embrace it.

"Why do they not teach you that time is a finger snap and an eye blink, and that you should not allow a moment to pass you by without taking joyous, ecstatic note of it, not wasting a single moment of its swift, breakneck circuit?"

– PAT CONROY

"'What day is it?'

'It's today,' squeaked Piglet.

'My favourite day,' said Pooh."

– A.A.MILNE

AN EXERCISE IN COLOR

Choose a color and decide to notice that color as you go about your day. Every time you notice the color, stop and acknowledge it. This will slow your thoughts and place you in the present moment.

"The secret of health for both mind and body is not to mourn for the past, worry about the future, or anticipate troubles, but to live in the present moment wisely and earnestly."

– BUDDHA

"When you have an intense contact of love with nature or another human being, like a spark, then you understand that there is no time and that everything is eternal."

– PAULO COELHO

DRIVE MINDFULLY

Driving becomes a habit; however, there is a lot that goes into it. Next time you go for a drive, be mindful of the sights around you. Turn off the radio. Become aware of the noise your car makes as you accelerate or decelerate, the way the air conditioner or heater feels against your skin, or any other sensation associated with driving. You will bring a renewed sense of calm to any car journey.

"Live with intention.
Walk to the edge.
Listen hard.
Practise wellness.
Play with abandon.
Laugh.
Choose with no regret.
Appreciate your friends.
Continue to learn.
Do what you love.
Live as if this is all there is."

– MARY ANNE RADMACHER

"Stop acting as if life is a rehearsal.
Live this day as if it were your last.
The past is over and gone.
The future is not guaranteed."

– WAYNE DYER

"The only true thing
is what's in front of
you right now."

– RAMONA AUSUBEL

BRUSH YOUR TEETH MINDFULLY

Today when you brush your teeth, pay attention to what you are doing. Feel your feet grounded on the bathroom floor. Notice the feeling of the bristles of the toothbrush on your gums, the sound of the brush against your teeth, the taste of the toothpaste, and the movement of your arm as you brush. Use all of your senses and as your mind wanders, bring it back to the sensations of brushing your teeth.

"Begin doing what you want to do now. We are not living in eternity. We have only this moment, sparkling like a star in our hand and melting like a snowflake."

– FRANCIS BACON SR.

"Looking at beauty in the world is the first step of purifying the mind."

– DR. AMIT RAY

"Compassion is not complete if it does not include oneself."

– ALLAN LOKOS

"There are only two ways to live your life. One is as though nothing is a miracle. The other is as though everything is a miracle."

– ALBERT EINSTEIN

"The past is the past and has nothing to do with you. It has nothing to do with right now. Do not let anything from your past inhibit you in this present moment. Start over. Start fresh. Each day. Each hour, if it serves you. Heck, each minute. Just get going."

– NEALE DONALD WALSCH

DECLUTTER

Set some time aside today to declutter an area of your home or workspace. Although it may seem overwhelming at first, doing this can actually be as peaceful as a meditation. Clutter is a way of holding onto the past, or fearing the future. Letting go of clutter is a way to live more mindfully and in the present.

"Clutter stops the flow of positive energy in your space and ultimately in your life."

– JAYME BARRETT

COMMUTE MINDFULLY

Instead of wishing the journey away, embrace the time that it has afforded you to sit and be. Be mindful of your emotions as they rise and fall, come and go. Recognise the frustration, anger, or impatience that may arise, but rather than thinking about them, judging them, or analysing them, simply acknowledge them.

"Rivers know this: there is no hurry. We shall get there some day."

– A.A. MILNE

"I deserve the best and I accept the best now."

– LOUISE HAY

INDIAN HEAD MASSAGE

Take 10 minutes today to give yourself a simple three-step Ayurvedic Indian head massage. First rub your temples with your fingertips in a gentle, circular pattern. For the second step, "shampoo" the scalp. Massage the entire scalp in small circles with gentle fingertips. Begin at the temples and move towards the back of the head. Finish by combing the scalp; place your fingertips at the hairline, and comb over the top of the head down towards the neck and shoulders.

"Breathe. Let go. And remind yourself that this very moment is the only one you know you have for sure."

– OPRAH WINFREY

"Listening is the way. Listening is the beginning of all progress."

– BRYANT MCGILL

BE MINDFUL
WITH MONEY

Living in the present means focusing on one financial decision at a time, as and when it arises. This will allow you to make a better decision about money, no matter how important. You can decide at that moment if it makes more sense to save or spend. So today, before you buy anything ask yourself: "Do I really need this? Should I spend this money right now or wait?"

"When you look at the sun during your walking meditation, the mindfulness of the body helps you to see that the sun is in you; without the sun there is no life at all and suddenly you get in touch with the sun in a different way."

– THÍCH NHẤT HẠNH

"It's not what you look at that matters, it's what you see."

– HENRY DAVID THOREAU

"What you think, you become. What you feel, you attract. What you imagine, you create."

– UNKNOWN

"What is life? It is the flash of a firefly in the night. It is the breath of a buffalo in the wintertime. It is the little shadow which runs across the grass and loses itself in the sunset."

– BLACKFOOT

"You've got this life and while you've got it, you'd better kiss like you only have one moment, try to hold someone's hand like you will never get another chance to, look into people's eyes like they're the last you'll ever see, watch someone sleeping like there's no time left, jump if you feel like jumping, run if you feel like running, play music in your head when there is none, and eat cake like it's the only one left in the world!"

- C. JOYBELL C.

"Like a child standing in a beautiful park with his eyes shut tight, there's no need to imagine trees, flowers, deer, birds, and sky; we merely need to open our eyes and realize what is already here, who we already are."

– BO LOZOFF

LAUGH

Laughing brings us into the present moment in a mindful way and
is a great stress reliever.

"The most wasted of all days is one without laughter."

– NICOLAS CHAMFORT

DANCE

Try a dance class — nothing brings your mind faster into the present moment than when you're trying to get your body to move to a rhythm.

STOLEN MOMENTS

The concept of wasted time does not exist for a mindful person. Every spare moment can be used for meditation. Feeling irritated while queuing at the post office, meditate on irritation. Sitting anxiously in the doctor's waiting room, meditate on your anxiety. Bored waiting at the bus stop, meditate on boredom. Try to stay alert and aware throughout the day. Be mindful of exactly what is taking place right now. Today, use every spare second to be mindful. Use all the moments you can.

"Your mind is your instrument. Learn to be its master and not its slave."

– REMEZ SASSON

MONOTASK

Do one thing at a time. There is a growing body of evidence that suggests multitasking makes us less efficient, less effective, more stressed, and more likely to make mistakes. Maintaining focus and interest on one task at a time is not easy, but start practising today.

"Today…spend more time with people who bring out the best in you, not the stress in you."

– UNKNOWN

"Smile, breathe,
and go slowly."

– THÍCH NHẤT HẠNH

"One day you will wake up and realize that life has passed you by, that your dreams of today are gone, that the things you wanted are no longer there. Not today. Not now. Not your life. This is the day where you take control and create your future. Life isn't about waiting, hoping or wishing. It is about creating, doing, and truly living. Today is that day."

– BRAD GAST

"There are far too many people who waste their time telling themselves that they don't have enough time."

– UNKNOWN

DON'T ANSWER YOUR PHONE IMMEDIATELY

Let it ring a couple of times as you collect your thoughts and prepare to answer. Think about the person calling. What do they look like? What frame of mind are they in?

HUGGING MEDITATION

You can practise this Buddhist hugging meditation with a loved one, or even with a tree. First bow to recognise the presence of each other and enjoy three deep, conscious breaths to bring yourself fully there. Open your arms and begin hugging, holding each other for three in-and-out breaths. With the first breath, be aware that you are present in this very moment and that you are happy. With the second breath, be aware that the other is present in this moment and that he or she is happy as well. With the third breath, be aware that you are here together, right now on this earth, and feel deep gratitude and happiness for that togetherness. Then release the other person and bow to each other to show thanks.

"Peace begins when expectation ends."

– SRI CHINMOY

TAKE A BATH

Today, take time out to wallow in a hot bath. Make your bathroom a haven of peace and calm. Banish your smart phone and light candles; use your favourite bubble bath or oil. Lie back and feel the warm water envelop your body. Focus on the sensations of warmth, inhale the scent of your bath products and observe how the candlelight reflects in the bubbles.

"In today's rush, we all think too much, seek too much, want too much and forget the joy of just being."

– ECKHART TOLLE

"Fear keeps us focused on the past or worried about the future. If we can acknowledge our fear, we can realize that right now we are okay. Right now, today, we are still alive, and our bodies are working marvellously. Our eyes can still see the beautiful sky. Our ears can still hear the voices of our loved ones."

– THÍCH NHẤT HẠNH

"Don't seek, don't search, don't ask, don't knock, don't demand — relax."

– OSHO

"We're all just walking each other home."

– RAM DASS

PEBBLE IN
YOUR POCKET

Such a simple thing, and yet something that Zen masters the world over do, is to keep a pebble in a pocket. Do this and each time you put your hand in your pocket, hold the pebble gently and let it serve as a reminder to pause, smile, and calmly breathe in and out.

"Write it on your heart that every day is the best day in the year."

– RALPH WALDO EMERSON

"The mind is everything.
What we think,
we become."

– BUDDHA

"Mindfulness is about being
fully awake in our lives.
It is about perceiving the exquisite
vividness of each moment.
We also gain immediate access to
our own powerful inner resources
for insight, transformation,
and healing."

– JON KABAT-ZINN

EXERCISE MINDFULLY

Exercising mindfully is an incredibly powerful stress reliever. When you're working out, be fully in the present moment. This is your time to focus completely on yourself. Bring awareness to your breath and the physical capabilities of your body. Feel every stretch deeply and commit to giving every move your all. When you focus on what you're doing, you improve the quality of your movement and, as a result, the quality of your overall workout. Feel your own strength and power as you exercise.

"Your vision will become clear only when you look into your heart. Who looks outside, dreams. Who looks inside, awakens."

– CARL JUNG

"Don't underestimate the value of doing nothing, of just going along, listening to all the things you can't hear, and not bothering."

– A.A. MILNE

LISTEN TO MUSIC

Really listen. Bring your attention to the sensations of sound and feeling as the piece begins. If your attention wanders, just gently remind yourself to return to the sounds and sensations of the music. If you can focus your mind entirely on that song and where it takes you, then you can transform your listening experience into a meditative experience.

"How we spend our days is of course how we spend our lives."

– ANNIE DILLARD

"Finish every day and be done with it.
You have done what you could.
Some blunders and absurdities,
no doubt, crept in.
Forget them as soon as you can,
tomorrow is a new day;
begin it well and serenely,
with too high a spirit to be cumbered
with your old nonsense."

– RALPH WALDO EMERSON

TRAFFIC LIGHT EXERCISE

Each time you have to stop at a red traffic light today, instead of being frustrated, use this still time to engage in a mindful practice. Bring focus to your breathing and give thanks for the car you are in, for the job you are driving to, or for the friend you are on your way to visit…

"Leave your front door and back door open. Let your thoughts come and go. Just don't serve them tea."

– SHUNRYŪ SUZUKI

CLEANING

When cleaning your home, notice any feelings of resistance and urges to get it done as quickly as possible. Then focus on the doing, not the getting done. The motion of simple tasks can make you more attentive and calm — the back and forth of the vacuum cleaner, for example. Chores can be meditative, just so long as you're not thinking about how much you hate them. There is much comfort and peace to be found in repetitive tasks.

"If you clean the floor with love, you have given the world an invisible painting."

– OSHO

"Forever is composed of nows."

– EMILY DICKINSON

"We have only now, only this single eternal moment opening and unfolding before us, day and night."

– JACK KORNFIELD

PICK A PROMPT TO REMIND YOU TO BE MINDFUL

Choose a cue that you encounter on a regular basis to shift your brain into mindful mode. For instance, you might pick a certain door you walk through or a picture on the wall, or use drinking tea or coffee as a reminder.

"To offer no resistance to life is to be in a state of grace, ease, and lightness."

– ECKHART TOLLE

"Perhaps ultimately, spiritual simply means experiencing wholeness and interconnectedness directly, a seeing that individuality and the totality are interwoven, that nothing is separate or extraneous. If you see in this way, then everything becomes spiritual in its deepest sense. Doing science is spiritual. So is washing the dishes."

– JON KABAT-ZINN